D0600614

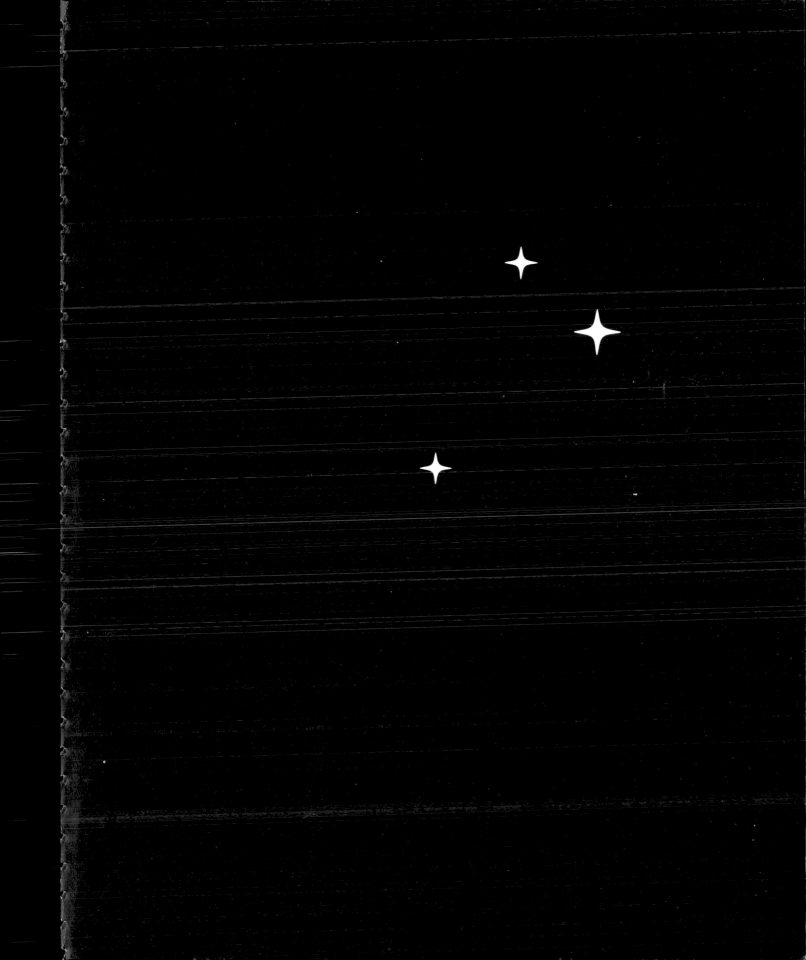

SPACE MISSION PATCHES

BY GREGORY L. VOGT

THE MILLBROOK PRESS ✳ BROOKFIELD, CONNECTICUT

Contents

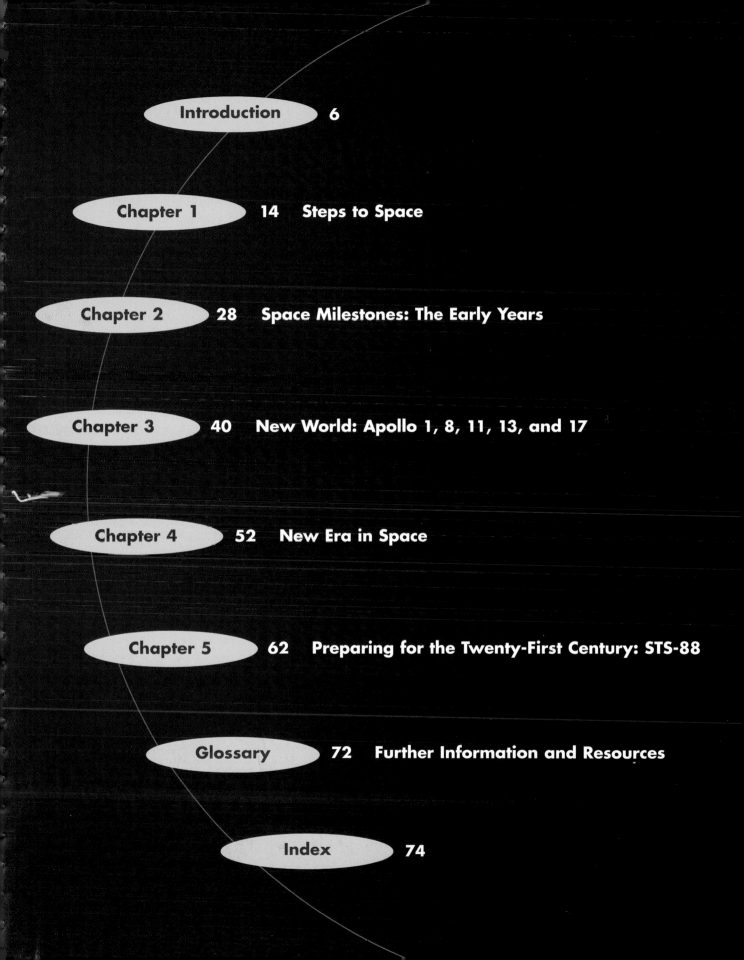

OCTOBER 29, 1998

A large crowd of well-wishers had gathered around the doors of the astronaut quarters at the National Aeronautics and Space Administration's (NASA) Kennedy Space Center at Cape Canaveral, Florida. It was a good day for a space launch and excitement was building. Three and a half miles away, the space shuttle *Discovery* was poised on the platform of the launch complex for the start of the STS-95 mission. *Discovery* was fully fueled and ready to accept its crew for its thunderous leap into space. A couple of hours before the scheduled liftoff, *Discovery*'s crew of seven astronauts appeared. They marched out proudly with big smiles and waves to the crowd. They were met with cheers and whistles. Television and still cameras whirred away. This was a historic moment.

NASA likes to think all its space launches are historic, but this one was especially so. The excitement centered about one crew member in particular who, at age 77, was 35 years older than *Discovery*'s mission commander, Curtis Brown. The crew member causing all the fuss was John H. Glenn Jr., a United States senator from the state of Ohio. Thirty-six years earlier, Glenn was an astronaut like the other crew members. In 1962, he became the first American astronaut to orbit Earth. Glenn circled Earth three times for a space ride total-

7

"pumpkin suits." If an emergency were to take place during launch, the suits would protect them from flames and from the stresses of parachuting to the ocean. The bright orange would enable rescue crews to spot them easily.

On the left shoulder of each suit was a flag representing the nation or space agency the astronaut came from. Five of the flags were the Stars and Stripes of the United States. A Japanese astronaut wore the red dot on a field of white representing the flag of Japan and a Spanish astronaut wore a patch with the flags of the nations represented by the European Space Agency. On the front of the suit, over the left breast, was a nametag, and below that was the patch of the National Aeronautics and Space Administration (NASA).

ing 4 hours and 56 minutes. Now, he was returning to space to conduct medical experiments on the nature and problems of aging. This flight would keep him in space for 135 orbits and 8 days and 22 hours.

It was not hard to spot the crew as they boarded a small bus for the short ride to the launch complex. Each wore bright orange launch-and-entry suits. The astronauts call their flight outfits

Space mission patches are colorful and fascinating to look at because they tell the story of space exploration.

It was a circular blue patch with the letters NASA stitched in white across the middle. Two red lines slashed diagonally across the patch and came together in a point in the upper right. The lines represented flight, one of NASA's major missions. A white line traced an ellipse (flattened circle) that enveloped the letters from the other direction. The ellipse represented a spacecraft in orbit around Earth. Finally, several small dots were scattered across the blue background to represent stars. Everyone who works at NASA fondly calls the patch the "meatball."

The Japanese and Spanish astronauts also had sim-ple rectangular patches of letters representing the names of their space agencies on their right shoulders. The Japanese patch read "NASDA" for the National Space Development Agency, and the patch for the Spanish astronaut read "ESA" for the European Space Agency.

The new patch is nicknamed the "vector" patch

Everybody who travels to space on the shuttle wears flags and space agency insignia on their flight suits. There is something else they wear as well. The STS-95 crew displayed a personal insignia, a patch that represented them and the mission they would fly on. Each shuttle crew has its own special patch that only they can wear to space. It is sewn on the right breast of their pumpkin suits.

The tradition of designing a special patch for space missions began early in the space program. Astronauts chose special symbols to represent their adventures. Space flight was and still is the greatest adventure of modern life. Although hundreds of astronauts have traveled to space and returned safely, space flight is not safe. Riding into space on a 700-foot pillar of flame is terribly dangerous and the space environment itself is so deadly that an unprotected human would perish in only a few seconds. Also dangerous is the fiery return through Earth's atmosphere back to Earth's surface.

Although the technicians who prepare the rocket and the engineers who control its flight try to make it as safe as possible, it still takes great courage to fly into space. The astronauts who travel there have to function as a team because their lives depend upon it. As they train for their mission, they bond together and become very special partners. Although it may seem insignificant to an outsider, the selection of their mission insignia or patch is an important step to space. It helps the crew build team spirit and trust for each other. A mission patch is a symbol of who the astronauts are and what they hope to accomplish during their journey in space.

Symbols are important to us, too, and have been so throughout history. The most powerful symbols we have represent beliefs. These are often our oldest symbols. Some, like crosses and six-pointed stars, represent religions. Colorful flags represent nations. Other symbols tell stories. Stick figure symbols carved in or painted on rock walls throughout the West represent the daily life and beliefs of the Native Americans who lived there a thousand years before. Elaborately painted coats of arms adorned the shields and armor breastplates worn in the middle ages by knights as they traveled eastward from Europe on the Crusades. Soldiers at war marched into battle behind a flag bearer carrying their nation's flag. No matter how badly the battle raged, the presence of their flag at the front of the advance spurred the soldiers on.

Today, we see symbols everywhere. A red, white, and blue flag waves in front of a school. A wild horse adorns the front of a racy sports car. A pair of golden arches announces a fast food restaurant. A swoosh mark is found emblazoned along the sides of athletic shoes. A computer has a rainbow-colored apple stuck to its side. A yellow seashell marks a gas station.

We use symbols for many things. While many symbols identify products, others give us directions. Black stick figures of men and women mark restroom doors. A red circle with a diagonal stripe over a picture of a cigarette tells people they shouldn't be smoking. A curved black arrow on a diamond-shaped yellow sign warns drivers of a curve in the road, and a red octagonal sign tells drivers to stop at the corner. A small black cross in a column of numbers is an instruction telling a student to add the numbers together.

The STS-95 Patch

Although we live in a world of symbols, we tend to take most of them for granted. The symbols we get excited about are those that represent dreams and adventures like the insignias for space shuttle missions. Space mission patches are colorful and fascinating to look at because they tell the story of space exploration.

The patch for the STS-95 mission and John Glenn's return to space consists of a large blue circle with a red border. The names of the crew are printed in yellow around the border. A gray space shuttle *Discovery* is shown rising over a light blue arc representing the line separating the sunlit side from the dark side of Earth. A large red 7 in the middle of the

12

patch represents the seven astronauts on the mission and the original seven Mercury astronauts. A small red Mercury space capsule circles *Discovery* and represents John Glenn's first flight. Finally, the colorful exhaust plumes from *Discovery*'s engines symbolize the major fields of science represented by the payloads of the STS-95 mission: microgravity (floating effect in space) and material science, medical research on humans, and astronomy.

The space shuttle *Discovery* remained in space for nearly nine days before returning to Earth on November 7, 1998. The crew performed many medical experiments with John Glenn as a test subject. They released and later captured a satellite that tested new equipment that could be used on the Hubble Space Telescope already in Earth orbit. They also studied the Earth and the Sun from space and performed a variety of science experiments. Except for a little nausea upon landing, the elderly John Glenn survived the flight in good form. Mission accomplished!

13

Chapter One

STEPS TO SPACE

In the early days of manned space flight, only two nations, the United States and the Soviet Union (now divided into several smaller nations including Russia) were sending people into space. Getting into space was a contest with serious implications. It was believed that the nation who could get there first and stay there permanently would have significant military and economic advantages over the other.

The Soviet Union won the first heat of the race by launching the first human. On April 12, 1961, Yuri Gagarin rocketed into space and orbited Earth one time before returning. He was followed into space less than a month later by American astronaut Alan B. Shepard Jr. Shepard rode in a Mercury space capsule perched on top of a Redstone rocket for a 15½-minute flight that reached space briefly and then parachuted into the Atlantic Ocean.

Five Mercury missions followed Shepard's flight. Each flight was more ambitious than the one before. At first, the purpose of reaching space was just to stay there, but during a speech given by President John F. Kennedy, the purpose was changed. Kennedy

Kennedy declared that the new goal of the American manned space program would be to land a man on the Moon and bring him back safely before 1970.

declared that the new goal of the American manned space program would be to land a man on the Moon and bring him back safely before 1970. It was a huge and seemingly impossible challenge, but the Mercury program fit right into the plan.

The Mercury missions helped scientists and engineers learn how to send humans safely into space and take care of their bodily needs, such as food, water, air, and waste removal, and temperature and pressure control. They learned how to control a spacecraft in orbit, communicate with Earth, take pictures and conduct scientific experiments, and bring astronauts back safely.

The longest Mercury mission lasted 34 hours and 9 minutes. This was not long enough to go to the Moon and back. Furthermore, the Mercury capsule held only one astronaut. A trip to the Moon would require two or three astro-nauts to do it safely. The Mercury program concluded in mid-May 1963. Almost two years later, Mercury was followed by the two-astronaut Gemini program.

Going to the Moon would involve a variety of risky space maneuvers that had never been tried before. It was decided early that sending one giant spacecraft to the Moon and back would be impracticable. The spacecraft would have to carry all of its remaining fuel to the Moon's surface and then launch it back above the Moon for powering the return trip. It would be much simpler if a small excursion craft actually landed on the Moon while a main ship with the return fuel remained in orbit. This meant that NASA would have to learn how to get two spacecraft to rendezvous in orbit and dock together. Rendezvous and docking became two of the primary missions of the Gemini program.

From March 1965 through November 1966, ten two-astronaut Gemini spacecraft rocketed to orbit on the top of Titan missiles. During this rapid series of space flights, the first spacewalks took place and spacecraft met in orbit and docked together. NASA scientists and engineers went to school on these missions. They learned the steps it would take to make the same things happen at the Moon.

Near the beginning of the Gemini program, the astronauts who flew the capsules to orbit decided it would be important for them to have a symbol of their dangerous adventure that they could wear on their flight suits. Coming from military backgrounds, it was only natural for the astronauts to think of cloth patches. The military services have used patches for a long time as a way of identifying both troops and special missions they train for.

The first space mission patches were simple symbols with crew names, mission numbers, and a special piece of artwork, such as a drawing of their spacecraft. The patches became a tradition that continues today.

NASA paused almost two years before launching the three-astronaut Apollo missions. The pause was longer than originally planned because of a tragic accident in which three astronauts perished inside a space capsule while training. NASA stopped the program while safety experts analyzed the cause of the accident. Corrections were made and the first Apollo crew flew into orbit in October 1968. A second crew traveled out to the Moon and circled around it before coming home. Two more missions tested equipment and techniques before the Apollo 11 crew landed on the Moon in July 1969. President Kennedy's goal of sending a man

safely to the Moon and back before the end of the decade was accomplished!

Six additional Apollo missions headed out for the Moon by the time the program ended in 1972. Because of malfunctions of the spacecraft, one of the crews had to abort the landing and make an emergency return to Earth.

The Apollo program was followed in 1973 with the launch of Skylab, NASA's first space station. The Skylab program borrowed a lot of the hardware used for the Apollo moon missions. The third stage of the Saturn 5 rocket to go to the Moon was converted to the space station and the three teams of astronauts that visited it rode Apollo space capsules to orbit. Skylab crews remained in space for as long as 84 days and accomplished a wide variety of scientific research while there.

One more Apollo-derivative mission took place in 1975. American astronauts and Soviet Union cosmonauts rendezvoused and docked in space. It was the first space mission involving international cooperation. The two nations that had feared each other and competed in the conquest of space now partnered together in a combined space mission. Although it would be many years before that kind of cooperation would happen again, the seed of future joint missions in space had been planted.

With the seeming peace between the space efforts of the United States and the Soviet Union, there was less urgency to go to space. Politicians in Washington began to look at the cost of space exploration and conclude that it was too expensive. NASA had to find ways to reach space more cheaply or they would find themselves out of business. The solution was to create a new kind of space vehicle that could be

19

Skylab, with Earth in the background

reused. The new vehicle was the space shuttle.

The space shuttle was supposed to cut the cost of space exploration by being only one tenth as costly to launch as a Saturn 5 rocket. It would have a large payload bay for carrying heavy and bulky satellites and spacecraft to orbit. It could be made ready to fly into space in only a few weeks after returning to Earth. Those goals were far tougher to accomplish than NASA had hoped, and it wasn't until April 1981 (exactly 20 years after Yuri Gagarin's flight) that the first shuttle lifted off to space. The flight lasted only two days. The shuttle was much more expensive to fly than planned and it took much longer to get ready than hoped—but it worked. Since the first shuttle flight, there have been more than a hundred space shuttle flights to orbit. Several have carried Russian astronauts and several times the

space shuttle has rendezvoused and docked with a giant Russian space station called *Mir*. Today, the shuttle is being used to carry to orbit the parts of a new space station called the International Space Station.

THE FIRST INSIGNIAS

None of the Mercury astronauts wore mission insignia on their silvery space suits during their flights. The practice of creating patches to represent space missions began during the Gemini flights. Mercury patches were created later to insure that all American space missions were represented. During his preparation for his second flight to space, John Glenn was asked why he didn't display his Mercury patch on various clothing astronauts wear during training. Shuttle astronauts frequently sew all of their mission patches on the blue flight suits they wear while flying high-

performance jet aircraft during training. Glenn explained that the Mercury patch held no meaning for him because he had no part in its creation and didn't wear it during his flight.

HOW MISSION INSIGNIAS ARE CREATED

The creation of a mission insignia or patch is both a simple and a complex process. In simple form, someone has an idea for what the

Each crew member has to agree that the patch represents the mission objectives and what each astronaut is trying to accomplish.

patch should look like and an artist draws it. The complex part comes in trying to get everyone to agree to it. Today, as many as seven astronauts ride to space on a single space shuttle mission. Each crew member has to agree that the patch represents the mission objectives and what each astronaut is trying to accomplish. If it stayed right there, the process would still be simple, but astronauts are excited about their upcoming missions. They want to share the adventure. Many family and neighborhood consultants are brought in for their expert opinions. Also, NASA managers have to agree that the insignias are appropriate and give them their approval, too.

The first mission patches were painted by hand by artists with brushes and paint on boards. As time went on, improvements in art technology led to changes in how the patches were designed. Artists began using airbrushes to paint the patches. Airbrushes are precisely controlled paint sprayers that artists can use to create fine details or to blend colors together over large areas of their work. The computer age has led to patches being created electronically with digital art programs. In addition to speeding up the creation of the initial design for a patch, computers permit quick and simple revisions of designs when all the consultant opinions come in. It isn't necessary to start from scratch just because the blue used on the patch is the wrong shade.

The patches designed for the Mercury through the Apollo mis-

23

sion were relatively simple affairs. They showed a representation of the mission, such as a design with the mission's number or a picture of the spacecraft. The patch for the first Moon landing shows a large eagle about to touch down on the Moon. *Eagle* was the name of the landing craft. Patches for the shuttle missions started out simple, too, but astronauts began requesting more and more complex designs. Their missions usually didn't involve something as spectacular as landing on the Moon. Astronauts wanted the lesser events of their flight to be represented, such as a spacewalk or the deployment of a satellite or a major science experiment.

A typical space shuttle patch starts with a crew meeting in which an artist is given some ideas by the crew. Sometimes the ideas are presented verbally and other times, the ideas are presented in the form of a rough sketch. One member of the crew is picked to work with the artist in the various stages of the patch design. Designating a crew contact member has really helped the artist get the job done. In early days, any crew member could call the artist and direct some changes to be made. Another crew member would call later and change the changes, and so on.

The artist takes the crew ideas and creates a color picture to show the crew how their ideas look all crammed together in a relatively small insignia. It is up to the artist to balance the elements—such as shuttle orbiter, the Sun or stars, and whatever else the crew wants—so that they are the right size next to each other. When completed, the first draft of the insignia is given to the crew for them to review and to seek family and neighbor opinions. Changes are requested, a new draft is created, and the review process is started over. This continues until everybody is happy.

The only rule for patch creation is that the patch has to be about 3 to 4 inches (about 7 to 10 centimeters) inches in size. It can be round, square, oval, or some other shape. Some have been shaped like a space capsule. The number of colors is limited to eight. This is because crew insignias are used on more things than just patches. The crew and NASA itself like to give out patches as souvenirs but patches are expensive. Less expensive to give out are vinyl decals. Printing the decals is where the rule of eight colors comes from. The decals are

Out of Sight

During a 1999 auction of space artifacts, a piece of the shoulder covering of the space suit worn by James Irwin while walking on the Moon during the Apollo 15 mission came up for bid. The piece featured the American flag patch and Irwin's name. The winning bidder paid $300,000 for it.

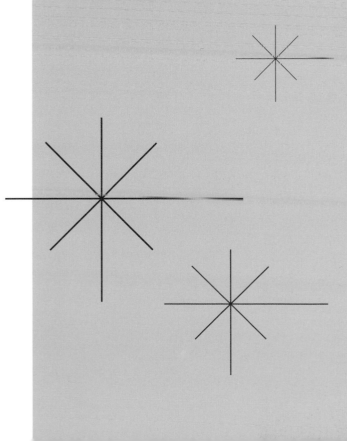

printed on white vinyl. Each color is produced from a pure ink color to get the sharpest reproduction. Insignia printers do not use the blended colors used in color magazine printing. (You can see the blending if you hold a magnifier over a magazine picture. Look for small dots in three or four colors that lay next to each other and blend to give a much wider range of color.) The printing presses that print the insignias cannot handle more than eight colors. The final stage in printing the decals is to cover the inks with varnish and then cut out the decals. Today's decals also come with a description of the symbols used printed on the peel-back paper on the adhesive side.

For the most part, astronaut crews design their own patches but several have been designed by famous space artists and even by a fashion designer. On one space shuttle mission, however, an astro-naut brought his nine-year-old son to the art department. The boy had drawn a mission patch for his dad's flight. The graphic artist was tickled to have the youngster sit next to him and serve as the patch's art director. When the boy said "Make that blue darker," the artist happily shifted the color on the computer monitor.

Collecting Space Flight Patches

Replicas of the patches worn by astronauts are popular collectible items that are easy to obtain. A list at the back of this book provides some distributors from whom patches can be purchased for a few dollars.

Some space patches are especially valuable because NASA will stow several packs of extra patches on space shuttle missions. These patches ride into space in a storage container and are retrieved after the space vehicle lands back on Earth. The patches are given away as actual space-flown mission souvenirs to people who helped make the missions possible. Some of these flown patches are mounted on a collection of pictures taken during the mission, called a mission montage. The patch lays on top of several pictures taken during the mission. The crew normally autographs dark areas on the pictures with metallic silver or gold ink. A small tag is added to the middle with an inscription thanking a specific person for his or her contribution to the mission. Other montages are given to schools or museums and the inscription briefly tells when the patch was flown in space and how many times it orbited Earth. Sometimes, a small U.S. flag that was also flown in space is attached to the montage. Mission montages are especially sought-after shuttle flight souvenirs.

Space-flown patches are more difficult and expensive to obtain than ordinary patch replicas. Someone who has received the patch from a flight crew has to be willing to sell it. Some space souvenir businesses have obtained these and other space-flown souvenirs, but the prices they charge for them will be considerably more than a few dollars. If you do plan to purchase these patches, it is important to obtain some documentation proving the patch was in space. Space-flown patches and ordinary patch replicas look exactly the same. Check on the Internet for distributors of space patches. Some of the Internet auction services such as eBay.com have space souvenir categories. Check the back of this book for information on where to obtain patches.

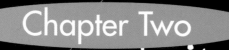

Chapter Two

SPACE MILESTONES: THE EARLY YEARS

As with every human endeavor, space exploration consists of many small steps and a few giant leaps. The small steps are important because they make the giant leaps, the milestones of space exploration, possible. The first space walks, for example, lasted only a few minutes but so much information was gained by the experiences that astronauts could confidently step down on the lunar surface several years later.

We now know that the Mercury program led to Gemini and then to Apollo, Skylab, and the present day space shuttle missions. Just what were those special steps that made the rest possible? Let's take a closer look.

GETTING THERE AND STAYING: MERCURY 3 AND 6

The first American step to space was a very small one by today's standard, but it was a giant leap back then. Rockets were extremely unreliable and very dangerous. They were as likely to explode or crash as they were to lift off skyward. A very brave military test pilot became the first American astronaut to fly into space. Alan B. Shepard Jr. donned a silvery spacesuit and rode a small elevator up a gantry (launch tower) next to a Redstone missile. Attached to the missile's top was a cone-shaped black Mercury space capsule. The capsule was so small that astronauts liked to

into his contour launch seat. The hatch was closed and bolted and Shepard anxiously waited for the countdown.

Alan Shepard wore only the NASA meatball patch on his spacesuit. Mission patches and flags would be added to later flights. The Mercury 3 patch, designed much later, nevertheless reveals the spirit of the mission. It is a small circle with a curved blue Earth at its bottom. Stretching over from the other side of Earth is the Florida peninsula where the launch took place. Three small arcing black lines represent the flight path of the rocket, and at their upper end is a small silvery Mercury capsule done in silver and black. The launch lines show that the capsule followed a short trip and landed in the ocean. The mission name and Shepard's last name are written in an arc across the patch top. The name of the capsule,

joke that you put it on rather than get into it.

The day was May 5, 1961, and the mission was called Mercury 3. No American had ever ridden a rocket to space, but a chimpanzee named Ham safely rode a similar space capsule and rocket four months earlier. With help from white-suited technicians, Shepard squeezed into the capsule hatch and strapped himself

Freedom 7, is written along the bottom.

It was thought that Shepard would get into the capsule and pop into space after a short countdown, but it didn't work out. Shepard remained on the launch pad for several hours. He soon became sorry he had had one more cup of coffee, because no one had thought to build a lavatory inside his space suit or capsule. There was not much he could do and when the countdown reached zero, Shepard made the first American flight into space with wet pants. That small detail would never be forgotten, and scores of astronauts now travel into space in comfort because of Shepard's sacrifice.

Shepard's flight lasted only 15 minutes and 22 seconds. His *Freedom 7* space capsule climbed to an altitude of 116.5 miles and parachuted back to Earth, where it landed in the Atlantic Ocean 303 miles from Florida. Shepard's rocket was not powerful enough to send *Freedom 7* into orbit, but the mission showed that astronauts could survive the launch and return safely.

A virtual repeat of Shepard's mission followed two months later and then it became John Glenn's turn to travel into space. Unlike Shepard, Glenn rode a much more powerful missile called the Atlas. The Atlas was capable of launching a Mercury space capsule to orbit. Glenn's mission patch, also designed after his flight, is a dark blue circle representing space. A curved Earth in light blue, for the ocean, and

Alan Shepard wore only the NASA meatball patch on his space-suit. Mission patches and flags would be added to later flights.

green, for the land, dominates the lower part of the patch. This time, white lines represent the path of flight. There are three lines for three orbits of Earth. Instead of the capsule, the word Friendship is shown at the end of the third orbit and a large number 7 lays behind the word. Across the top is the mission name, Mercury 6, and Glenn's last name is written along the bottom. The numbers on the patch are a little confusing. The 7 on all the Mercury mission patches refers to the num-ber of American astro-nauts chosen for space flight. The 6 on Glenn's patch means that this is the sixth Mer-cury capsule launch.

John Glenn's launch was a frustrating one. Many times Glenn suited up and climbed into the capsule only to have to climb out because of some problem or another that caused engineers to delay the flight. The weather at the launch site was stormy on many days and Glenn was get-ting impatient for his adventure. Finally, on February 20, 1962, Glenn got the ride of his life. The Atlas rocket lunged upward in a huge cloud of white smoke. The acceleration of his rocket pushed him back into his launch seat and he felt many times his own weight. Soon, Glenn reached orbit.

Everything was going great. The view of Earth below was "tremendous." Glenn reported that he felt fine in weightlessness. Then, problems began to crop up. The autopilot control system began to malfunction and Glenn had to take manual control. Small thrusters were used for steering the Mercury capsule in space. The autopilot system was causing the thrusters to fire in ways they shouldn't. While Glenn was controlling his capsule manually, mission engineers on Earth received a signal from the capsule that the landing bag was not locked into place. Just before splashing down into the ocean, a rubber bag on the capsule bottom would inflate and this would cushion the impact. If the bag were not locked, that meant that the heat shield on the capsule would not do its job and Glenn could burn up on reentry into Earth's atmosphere.

Glenn was instructed to leave a small cluster of rocket engines on the outside of the heat shield in place during reentry. Normally, after slowing the capsule, the cluster would be jettisoned. The engineers hoped the pack would hold the heat shield in place so that Glenn would be safe. Glenn made his reentry and landed safely in the ocean. It was later learned that the signal itself was the problem. It had malfunctioned and Glenn was never in any danger.

John Glenn's mission proved that astronauts could survive in space for many hours and perform useful work while up there. Three additional Mercury missions followed and each stayed in space longer than the ones before. One of the seven astronauts did not get to fly during the Mercury program. Donald K. Slayton was grounded due to potential heart problems. Slayton returned to flight status many years later for the Apollo-Soyuz mission.

PRACTICING FOR THE MOON: GEMINI 4, 5, AND 7/6

Now NASA was aiming squarely at the Moon. To get there, astronauts would have to be able to take space walks, remain in space for long periods, and rendezvous and dock their spacecraft. The ten Gemini missions enabled them to learn how to do those things. Three of the missions, in particular, pioneered important skills that the other missions later developed. For example, Gemini 4 pioneered space-

walking. The extravehicular activity (EVA) lasted only 22 minutes. Follow-up missions had EVAs that lasted up to five and a half-hours.

It was during the Gemini missions that the tradition of mission patches started. Up until then, all spacecraft were given names such as *Liberty Bell 7* or *Faith 7*. The first Gemini capsule (*Gemini 3*) was unofficially nicknamed Molly Brown. (NASA didn't officially name any of the Gemini capsules.) The name was derived from the musical play *The Unsinkable Molly Brown*, about a survivor of the *Titanic*. Virgil I. Grissom was one of two astronauts to ride the first Gemini to orbit. Grissom's Mercury flight was in a space capsule named *Liberty Bell 7*. After splashdown, the capsule sunk in the Atlantic Ocean. Grissom didn't want a repeat of the mishap and named the capsule Molly Brown. NASA decided to stop the process of naming space capsules and the flight crews resorted to designing mission patches. Naming spacecraft was started again during the Apollo program but the mission patch tradition continued.

Gemini mission patches are relatively simple designs. Most feature spacecraft or stars, but a few have symbols that require explaining. Gemini 4's patch, designed later, is red, with a picture of a Gemini space capsule in white and a white-suited spacewalker attached to the capsule with a gold tether line. Words on the patch read "Gemini 4, First Spacewalk," and the last names McDivitt and White.

The June 1965 flight of Gemini 4 lasted almost four days. At the time, this was the longest space flight in the American space program. On board were astronauts James A. McDivitt and Edward H. White

II. The Gemini capsule they rode in looked something like the black Mercury capsule, but it was larger—to fit two people—and there was a white extension on the blunt end where rocket fuel, cooling systems, drinking water, and communications equipment were kept. The white storage section would be jettisoned on reentry; only the capsule would make it to splashdown in the ocean.

The big event of Gemini 4 was the spacewalk by Ed White. Both astronauts put on white space suits and a hatch was opened for White to wiggle out of. As shown on their mission patch, White remained attached to the Gemini space capsule by a gold tether. The purpose of the tether was to keep White from floating away and to deliver oxygen for him to breathe. White quickly found out that it was difficult to move about in space and that perspiration fogged his space helmet. Nevertheless, much was learned about venturing outside space capsules and future spacewalkers had an easier time because of White's experience.

The tradition of mission patches started with the Gemini 5 flight.

The central feature of the Gemini 5 patch is a covered wagon. One of the objectives of the mission was to remain in space for eight days. The covered wagon symbol harkened back to the pioneer days when people put signs on their wagons reading "California or Bust." For Gemini 5, the motto written on the patch was "Eight Days or Bust." This motto caused some disagreement because the NASA administrator at the time, James Webb, thought the motto could be a problem. If the mission failed to last eight days, people would think the mission busted. Webb was also concerned with how the motto would translate into other languages in newspaper stories around the world. The actual patches worn by the

Astronaut Edward H. White II, floats in space during the Gemini 4 mission

37

patch is mostly black with Roman numerals VII (7) and the last names Lovell and Aldrin. The black represents space and a gold crescent represents the Moon. In the middle of the patch is a Gemini space capsule.

NASA ran into some problems with the Gemini 6 mission. The plan was to send Walter M. Schirra Jr. and Thomas P. Stafford to rendezvous in space with an Agena rocket booster launched a few days earlier. NASA couldn't get the Agena into space and the Gemini 7 mission with Frank Borman and James A. Lovell Jr., was launched instead. Gemini 6 followed later and used the orbiting Gemini 7 as the target. Both launches took place in December 1965. Gemini 7 reached orbit on December 4.

Gemini 5 crew had small pieces of white cloth sewn over the "eight days or bust" words to avoid problems. After the success of the mission, the words were restored to the patch.

Gemini 6's black patch is in the shape of a hexagon (six-sided figure). The flight path for the space capsule on the patch is in the shape of a 6. The Gemini 7

This was planned to be a very long mission to give astronauts the experience of being in space long enough to go to the Moon and back. Borman and Lovell had to sit in their space capsule for nearly 14 days. It was tight in there. They had about the same amount of room as in the front seat of a small sports car. The two conducted scientific experiments, practiced space navigation and maneuvering, ate food, and communicated with Earth. Seven hours after Gemini 6 reached orbit on December 15, the two space capsules came within a few feet of each other. The astronauts jokingly complained about traffic jams in space.

Other Gemini missions also practiced rendezvousing and even the docking of two spacecraft in orbit. There were more science experiments and longer spacewalks. The last Gemini flight took place in November 1966. NASA was almost ready to go to the Moon. That would be the job of the Apollo program.

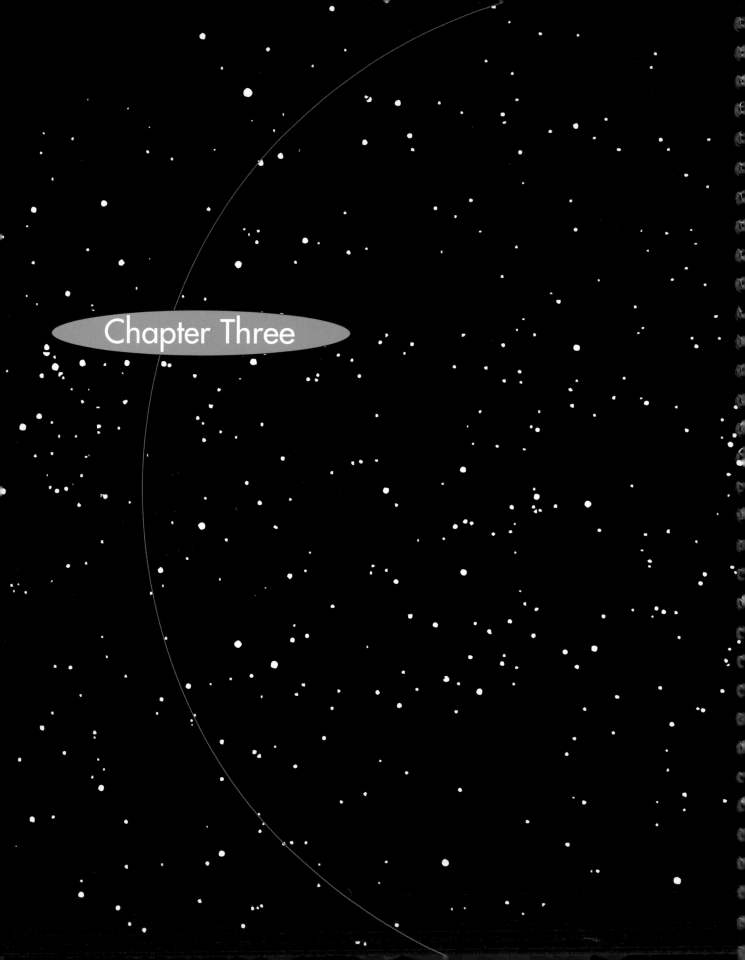

Chapter Three

NEW WORLD:
APOLLO 1, 8, 11, 13, AND 17

There seemed to be no stopping NASA's march to the Moon. As one after another Gemini mission clicked off success, the giant Saturn V rocket that would carry humans on their greatest adventure was nearly ready. A four-legged landing craft was under construction as well, and a new space capsule was undergoing tests. The bell-shaped capsule, called the command module, was large enough for three astronauts. It would be attached to a cylindrical service module that would provide the rocket power for entry into lunar orbit and for the trip home.

The first flight test of Apollo was to be Apollo 1 with the crew of Virgil Grissom, Roger Chaffee, and Edward White. Their mission patch gives no hint of what actually happened. The Apollo 1 patch is a series of concentric circles. The round patch begins first as an American flag, but this is overlaid with a gold ring with the last names of the three crew members and the name "Apollo 1." In the center of this ring is a partial Earth with the southeastern United States, Central America, and northern South America shown in gold threads. Blue represents the Atlantic and Pacific Oceans and the Gulf of Mexico. Just at the horizon of Earth is a half Moon in gold surrounded by black for space. Perched over the ocean is a white Apollo command and service module.

Apollo 1 was scheduled as a flight test in Earth orbit, but it was a

BORMAN LOVELL ANDERS

The Apollo 8 patch

the fire was corrected and other potential safety problems were fixed. On October 11, 1968, NASA returned to space with the Apollo 7 mission. Apollo 8 followed in December. The patch for that mission clearly tells the mission story. The patch is in the shape of a rounded triangle. Resting in a field of dark blue is a full Earth with North America at its center. Much smaller and above Earth is a Moon of gold and silver. Surrounding the two planetary bodies is an orange figure 8 that is drawn to make it appear that it is stretching back into the patch. At the bottom of the 8 the names Borman, Lovell, and Anders are sewn in white thread. Apollo 8 was a 6-day mission in which Frank Borman, James A. Lovell Jr., and William A. Anders traveled from the Earth to the Moon. On arriving at the Moon, their spacecraft went into

mission never to be. On January 27, 1967, the crew was running a simulation of their mission inside their space capsule. A fire broke out in the capsule that burned furiously in the oxygen atmosphere inside the capsule. The second American astronaut to travel to space, the first American space walker, and a space flight rookie died in seconds.

The tragedy caused the American space program to stand down for 18 months while the cause of

lunar orbit for 20 hours as the crew photographed potential landing sites. They then returned to Earth in a maneuver that looked like a large figure 8.

Two more Apollo missions tested spacecraft systems and space navigation. By July 1969, NASA was ready to try for the first landing. Neil A. Armstrong and Edwin E. Aldrin Jr. were picked for the crew that would actually set foot on the Moon. Michael Collins would remain in the command module in lunar orbit.

By this time, NASA permitted the naming of spacecraft again. The command module was named *Columbia* and the lander named *Eagle*. The mission patch is very clear in its intent. A gold border surrounds a field of black upon which is sewn a small planet Earth and the name "Apollo 11" in gold. At the bottom of the patch is a blue lunar surface with several craters. Just about to land on the

Moon is a bald eagle with its wings spread and an olive branch held in its talons. The olive branch is a universal symbol of peace.

On July 16, 1969, the Saturn 5 rocket carrying the Apollo 11 crew thundered into life. Its five first-stage engines generated 7.5 million pounds of thrust, causing the 36-story-tall rocket to creep upward, slowly at first, and then accelerate faster and faster. In only minutes, the crew reached Earth orbit. The Apollo command

The Apollo 11 Patch

and service modules and the landing craft were still attached to the rocket's third stage. At the right moment, the third stage fired, accelerating the astronauts to a rendezvous with the Moon three days later.

Traveling to the Moon took lots of faith on the part of the astronauts. They aimed their spacecraft not at the Moon but at a point in space where the Moon would be three days later.

They also had to arrive at the right speed and angle so that the engines on the service module could slow the spacecraft enough for the Moon's gravity to capture the module in orbit. The three-day trip across 225,000 miles of space was uneventful, but excitement about the landing captured the attention of the entire world.

On July 20, Armstrong and Aldrin fired the main engine on their landing craft so that it would drop out of orbit. Unlike landing on Earth, in which parachutes or airplane wings could be used to slow the vehicle, landing on the Moon required rocket engines. The Moon has no air to slow visitors down. The *Eagle* landing craft performed well, although computer overloads caused a few worrisome alarms. Near the Moon's surface, the crew spotted large boulders in their planned landing site and they had to maneuver their lander to a smoother place. With only a few seconds of fuel left, they touched down safely. Armstrong radioed Earth that the "Eagle has landed."

After a rest period, first Armstrong and then Aldrin climbed down the ladder attached to one of

44

the lander's four legs. For two and a half-hours, they bounded about on the low-gravity surface of the Moon, collected rocks and sediment samples, set up experiments, and took pictures. The same lander leg with the ladder had a plaque attached to it that read "We came in peace for all mankind." The crew left a gold replica of the olive branch on their mission patch on the Moon as well as an Apollo 1 patch in tribute to their lost comrades.

There were six additional Apollo flights to the Moon but only five actually landed. Apollo 13 was a jinxed mission. The crew wanted something different for their patch. They chose an artistic treatment of a chariot crossing the sky with the mythical god Apollo. The design also included Earth, Moon, and the Sun. As the design progressed, the chariot was dropped and replaced by three flying horses. The crew also dropped their names from the patch and instead added the Latin words *Ex Luna, Scientia*, or "from the Moon, knowledge."

Unfortunately, the Apollo 13 mission returned little information from the Moon. On the way there, an oxygen tank in the service module of their spacecraft exploded. The crew lost their main engine for return from the Moon, much of their electrical power, energy for keeping the space capsule warm, and much of their breathing oxygen.

The Apollo 13 patch

as possible. Apollo 13 turned into a miserable trip but had a very happy ending. The explosion did not damage the Apollo capsule and they successfully used it to splash down into the Pacific Ocean nearly six days after they lifted off.

In rapid succession, Apollo 14, 15, and 16 successfully landed on the Moon. Each mission was more ambitious than the one before. The final Apollo mission was number 17. The lunar surface crew, Eugene A. Cernan and Harrison H. Schmitt, made three moonwalks for a total of 22 hours, collecting samples and taking pictures. With the assistance of an electric vehicle, first used on Apollo 15, the crew covered 21.75 miles of lunar surface.

Since they were still on the way to the Moon when this happened, they had to use the Moon's gravity to swing them back toward Earth. The crew climbed into the landing craft that still had power and life support.

For a time, the crew was fine, but the lander craft was designed for two and power and oxygen were running out. In the last hours before reentry into Earth's atmosphere, the crew had to endure freezing temperatures and conserve power and oxygen as much

Crew ideas for their mission insignia were also ambitious and eventually they asked space artist Bob McCall to help them out. After several concepts, including a patch that had a portrayal of Stonehenge

46

in England, a design was created that represented the crew. The circular patch has a silver border with the name "Apollo 17" and the last names of the crew members separated by stars. A gold bust of Apollo represents the program and the intelligence, wisdom, and ambition of humankind. Behind Apollo is the outline of an American eagle. The eagle's wings have Stars and Stripes to represent the American flag. The wings just touch the lunar surface near the top of the patch. Finally, in the dark background of space is the planet Saturn and a spiral galaxy that represents space exploration goals of the future.

CLOSER TO HOME: SKYLAB AND APOLLO-SOYUZ

As NASA wound down the Apollo Moon program, the space agency came under criticism. People were becoming bored with TV coverage of astronauts on the Moon. Six landings seemed excessive. What were people getting out of the billions of dollars spent to make the landings possible? NASA tried to explain that learning about the Moon helped us learn about Earth. Rocks brought home were 3 to 4 billion years old. Scientists were using them to learn about the origins of the solar system. The rocks also let scientists peek at the composition of the Moon so that future colonists on the Moon would know what resources were available to them. NASA also explained that the space program led to many jobs on Earth and that space research led to new products from such mundane things as better ballpoint pens to advanced medical technology. Still, people and their elected leaders complained. They said we should be doing more for Earth, and that we should work with other nations to share the cost

of space exploration. NASA's next two space ventures did just that.

Science fiction writers had long written about space stations in Earth orbit where scientists could do long-term research and study Earth from above. Using a modified third stage of the Saturn 5 Moon rocket, NASA built its first space station. The station was called *Skylab* and it was launched to Earth orbit on May 14, 1973. The launch was nearly a disaster. One of the heat and micrometeoroid shields along the side of the space station was ripped off by air rush shortly after liftoff. One of two large solar panels (large winglike surfaces covered with solar cells to make electricity from sunlight) opened when it shouldn't have and ripped off as well. Its twin panel tried to open, too, but some twisted metal caught it. Skylab made it to orbit but was clearly wounded. Without its main solar panels working, the station was short of electrical power. The missing shield caused the station to get much hotter inside than it was supposed to. If Skylab were to be used, astronauts would have to repair it.

The first crew to arrive at Skylab set out to repair the damage. The mission insignia shows no hint of the repair mission. Instead, the patch represents the crew's commitment to do scientific research. A

48

The patches
for all
four Skylab
missions

black-and-white border on the circular patch surrounds a black silhouette of Skylab with all its parts intact. Beneath the station is Earth and its picture represents the crew's work to study Earth from space. Behind Earth is the Sun but all that is seen is the Sun's atmosphere. Earth creates an eclipse. Study of the Sun was another major goal of the flight The words on the patch read "Skylab 1" and the last names of Pete Conrad, Joseph P. Kerwin, and Paul J. Weitz.

The first Skylab crew remained 28 days in orbit. This was the longest space flight to date. They freed the stuck solar panel and erected a parasol over the missing

shield. The next crew arrived a few months later and stayed for 59 days. The Skylab 2 patch is mostly red, white, and blue. The central feature is a representation of the picture of a man drawn by Leonardo Da Vinci more than 500 years earlier. The picture illustrates the proportions of the human form and highlights the study of the human body in weightlessness. Behind the man is a circle that is half Earth and half the Sun. Again, this represented the main emphasis of the Skylab program—Earth and solar study. The patch words read "Skylab II" and the last names of Alan Bean, Owen K. Garriott, and Jack R. Lousma.

Skylab's third mission broke all space flight endurance records by remaining in space for 84 days.

The final Skylab crew chose a rounded triangle for their patch shape. In the center are three circles. In one circle is a tree, symbolizing our natural environment and how the mission would advance the study of Earth's resources. The second circle features a hydrogen atom, representing exploration of the physical world and our use of technology. The third circle has the shape of a man, which represents the Skylab medical studies. Surrounding the third circle is a rainbow, based on the rainbow of the Bible. The rainbow embraces the man and extends to the tree and the atom. This demonstrates the crew's belief that humans bring together technology and nature. The crew for Skylab 3 was Gerald P. Carr, Edward G. Gibson, and William R. Pogue. Their last names appear on the blue background of the patch along with the word "Skylab."

Skylab's third mission broke all space flight endurance records by remaining in space for 84 days. By the end of the program, the three Skylab crews amassed more than 45,000 pictures of Earth from space and 177,000 pictures of the Sun. They spent close to a thousand hours in medical and other research.

The first era of American space flight closed with the 1975 Apollo-Soyuz mission. Soviet cosmonauts Aleksey Leonov and Valeriy Kubasov rocketed to orbit in a Soviet Soyuz space capsule. Seven hours later, American astronauts Tom Stafford, Vance Brand, and Donald K. Slayton followed in an Apollo space capsule. Two days later, the two spacecraft ren-

50

dezvoused in orbit and docked. It was the first docking of spacecraft from two different nations. For two days, the crews shared living space and meals and participated in joint scientific research. As far as space research goes, this flight wasn't very important. Its importance was that it demonstrated that nations could work together in space and it pioneered the use of docking adapters that could be used to join different spacecraft in orbit. The fruit of this mission would not be realized until many years later.

The circular patch for the Apollo-Soyuz mission features a red border surrounding a gold ring in which the five astronauts' last names were stitched. A small section of blue in the border has three white stars for the American astronauts and a small red section has two stars for the Soviet cosmonauts. The center

of the patch shows the two spacecraft about to dock over Earth, with the Sun in the background. The American crew designed the official mission insignia but the Soviets had their own patch that was also used. It is circular with intertwining red and blue swirls that have "Apollo" and "Soyuz" written in the Cyrillic alphabet. In Russian, *soyuz* means "union." The center of the patch has a disk with the two joined spacecraft over a white Earth.

The Apollo-Soyuz patch

Chapter Four

NEW ERA IN SPACE

After the Apollo-Soyuz mission, six years passed before the United States returned astronauts to space. When they lifted off, they rode a new kind of space vehicle—the space shuttle. The shuttle began a new era in space flight. Instead of building an expendable rocket for each space flight, the shuttle was reusable. The space capsule, called an orbiter, was really an airplane that flew to orbit as a rocket and glided back to a runway as an airplane. Boosting the orbiter to space were two solid rocket boosters that were strapped to the side of a big fuel tank that contained liquid oxygen and hydrogen for the three main engines on the orbiter. When their fuel was consumed, the solid rocket boosters returned to the ocean by parachute for retrieval and reuse. The only thing not used again was the fuel tank.

THE EARLY MISSIONS: STS-1 AND 9, 41-C AND 51-L

Exactly twenty years to the day after the Soviet cosmonaut Yuri Gagarin became the first human to travel to space, the first space shuttle lifted off. The vehicle was named the *Columbia*, after an old sailing ship. Onboard *Columbia* were astronauts John Young of Gemini and Apollo fame and new astronaut Robert Crippen. The flight was simply a test of the space shuttle concept and it lasted only two days. NASA wanted to prove that a rock-

are the name *Columbia* and the crew's last names. These are placed over a picture of Earth, and flying around Earth is a space shuttle orbiter. The patch was designed to show how the space shuttle would work.

The first few space shuttle missions were further tests of the system. One of the important things about the orbiter's design was a 60-foot-long payload bay in its back. In space, long doors open to expose the payload carried inside. The payload might be a satellite to be popped into orbit or a spacecraft to be sent on to another planet. On the STS-9 mission that was launched at the end of 1983, the payload was a large cylindrical science laboratory called Spacelab.

The Spacelab enlarged the working space for the astronaut crew. There was room for many pieces of scientific equipment along

et airplane could safely carry astronauts to orbit and land them on a runway back on Earth.

The first space shuttle flight was called STS-1, which meant Space Transportation System flight 1. Young and Crippen's patch is fairly simple in design. It features a triangular area with a space shuttle rocketing upward. Below the rocket

54

its walls, floor, and ceiling. During the flight, the crew of six astronauts conducted 73 experiments.

The STS-9 patch is a rounded vertical rectangle with the crew names in a red border. *Columbia*, with its payload bay doors open and Spacelab visible, is located in the patch center. *Columbia* is drawn to look as if it was coming out of the patch. Earth is behind the orbiter and nine stars in the background represent STS-9. A blue and white swirl around Earth portrays the orbit of STS-9. At the bottom of the patch is a white banner that reads "*Columbia*" and "*Spacelab 1.*"

One after another shuttle missions flew to orbit. Three more orbiters were added to the fleet. They were called *Challenger*, *Discovery*, and *Atlantis*. Again, each was named after a famous sailing vessel.

Starting with the tenth shuttle flight, NASA decided to change the numbering system of the flights. The tenth flight was called 41-B. The 4 stood for 1984. The 1 meant the launch was to take place from the Kennedy Space Center in Florida (a second launch site was being built in California and would be called 2). The B meant the flight was the second flight scheduled for the year.

The STS-9 patch

MERBOLD • PARKER • YOUNG • SHAW • GARRIOTT • LICHTENBERG

Columbia • Spacelab 1

The 41-C mission in 1984 was especially exciting. A scientific satellite called *Solar Max* was ailing. Scientists needed the data it could provide to help them learn about the Sun. The satellite had worked for a time but now it was malfunctioning. Normally, the satellite would be written off, but the space shuttle gave NASA the opportunity to repair the satellite.

After arriving in orbit, the space shuttle *Challenger* was maneuvered to rendezvous with the satellite. Two astronauts, George Nelson and James van Hoften, put on spacesuits and went out into *Challenger*'s payload bay. They strapped on rocket propulsion devices that enabled them to fly out from the bay and capture the satellite so that it could be repaired. Their repair work was successful and the satellite was released to go on gathering data about the Sun.

The 41-C patch is circular with a border with the names of the crew. The inside circle of the patch is actually the outline of a space helmet. On the face of the helmet is a picture showing part of Earth at the top, *Challenger* to the left, an astronaut capturing *Solar Max*, and a yellow Sun with large rays. One other object is shown on the patch. This is a drawing of the Long Duration Exposure Facility. LDEF, as it was called, was a laboratory to be left in space. Various materials were placed on and in LDEF to see how they would survive exposure in space for many months.

By the time of the 51-L mission, space shuttle flights got out of order. There were many delays for some missions and others flew earlier than originally scheduled. Instead of being the twelfth flight manifested for 1985, 51-L became the first flight of 1986.

The crew of seven astronauts included a high school teacher named Christa McAuliffe. Their insignia shows a planet Earth with the orbiter *Challenger* launching from Florida and swinging around Earth. Instead of a black or dark blue space background, the sky is a partial American flag with seven stars and several red and white stripes. Crossing in front of the flag is a silver comet. The crew expected to observe Haley's Comet from orbit. Next to McAuliffe's name at the bottom of the patch is an apple to represent a teacher in space.

Liftoff took place on January 28, 1986. Just over one minute into the flight, the vehicle exploded. The crew was lost. The nation and the world were stunned at the tragedy. As it had after the tragic loss of the Apollo 1 crew many years earlier, the space program stood down for a period of rebuilding. Many safety problems were discovered and corrected. Work on the second launch site was discontinued.

Two years later, the space shuttle *Discovery* returned to space and exploration began again. The missions were named by the old STS system again. Thus, the return flight was named STS-26. A replacement orbiter was constructed and named *Endeavour*.

ROUTINE SPACE FLIGHT STS-61

As NASA regained its confidence, space missions became more and more ambitious. New missions

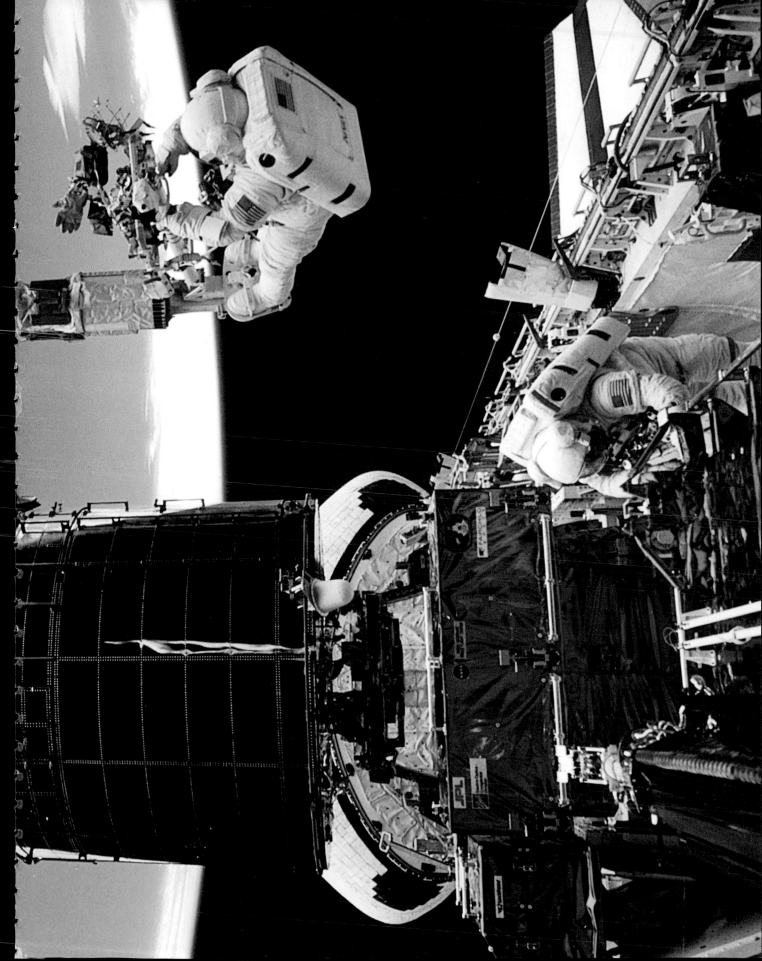

able to see deeper and more clearly into space than any telescope on Earth. It would revolutionize astronomy. Unfortunately, a mistake was made when the giant mirror in the telescope was manufactured. The error was tiny but it made it difficult for the telescope to focus its images.

The world of astronomy was devastated by the focus problem but eventually a solution was found. Designers of the Hubble Space Telescope planned to have it periodically visited by the space shuttle so that new instruments could replace old and repairs be made. The solution to the problem was to add corrective lenses to the telescope during a repair mission. In other words, the Hubble Telescope was to get glasses.

The repair mission fell to the crew of the STS-61 flight in December 1993. Seven astronauts

were flown to learn about the effects of weightlessness on all sorts of animals and on chemical reactions. Experiments were flown to study crystal formation, the human body, objects in deep space, and Earth and its oceans and atmosphere. One mission in particular caught the attention of the world. In April 1990, the crew of STS-31 launched the Hubble Space Telescope. From its orbit around Earth, the telescope was supposed to be

rocketed to orbit and rendezvoused with the Hubble Space Telescope. One astronaut used the shuttle's robot arm to capture the spacecraft and mount it in the payload bay of space shuttle orbiter *Endeavour*. Over the next several days, the crew made five spacewalks to fix the telescope's vision and replace worn or defective parts. Four astronauts, working in teams of two, alternated days of space walking with rest. By the time the mission was over, the Hubble Space Telescope's vision was restored and the spacecraft became a space discovery machine that opened the farthest reaches of the universe to exploration.

The STS-61 astronauts were confident of their ability to fix the telescope and what it would accomplish after it had been repaired. They expressed this confidence on their mission patch. It is a circle with crew names along the border. The astronaut symbol, three converging rays meeting at a five-pointed star and a ring to represent an orbit, cross the middle of the patch. In the very center of the patch is a gold circle with rays of light focused on a larger circle below. The two circles represent the mirrors of the Hubble Space Telescope and how light would be collected by it. A blue background holds stars, planets, and galaxies for the telescope to study.

The STS-61 patch

Chapter Five

PREPARING FOR THE
TWENTY-FIRST CENTURY: STS-88

The switch from expendable rockets to the reusable space shuttle in 1981 signaled the start of a second era in space travel. The first era explored the frontiers of space flight and discovered that humans could survive there. The second era pioneered routine space flight. Now, a third era has begun. In this era, humans will go to space to stay. The United States, Russia, and 14 other nations of the world are constructing an International Space Station that crews will occupy continuously for ten years or more. In space, scientists will conduct long-term research on both living and nonliving things and it is hoped that new discoveries made there will lead to such advances as cures for diseases, improved food production techniques, and better monitoring of Earth's environment.

STS-88

Construction of the International Space Station has already begun. Parts of the station are in orbit waiting for other pieces to be launched and assembled. When completed, the station will be nearly the size of two football fields and weigh almost a million pounds.

The first station component was launched to orbit by the Russians in 1998. It was originally called the FGB, or functional cargo block, but it was given a new name for the flight. The FGB is now known as *Zarya*, which means "sunrise" in Russian. Following *Zarya* came the

63

A view from STS-88 of the Russian FGB, also called *Zarya*

first American launch to the station. The STS-88 crew carried a node, called *Unity*, that will be used for linking together station parts. More than 35 future launches will carry more parts to be joined to the node. Eventually, the station will consist of more than one hundred components, including several cyl-indrical modules for living and conducting scientific research. Large solar panels with solar cells for making electricity will extend outward to capture the Sun's rays. There will also be a long beam that a large robot arm will move along to handle payloads and other objects.

To commemorate their mission, the STS-88 crew designed a circular patch showing the space shuttle with the *Unity* module in its payload bay and the robot arm grasping the *Zarya*. In the background is a rising Sun that symbolizes the dawning of a new era of international cooperation in space. Also in the background is the Big Dipper constellation pointing to the North Star, which has served as a guiding light for generations.

BEYOND EARTH

Like the Redstone rocket that lifted Alan Shepard into space 40 years ago, the International Space Station is just a stepping stone. The next step will take humans to the Moon to stay, then to Mars, and then beyond. What will their mission patches look like?

Space mission insignias or patches are like a history book.

Taken individually, they are colorful souvenirs of space exploration and make great collectibles. Taken as a group, they symbolically tell the story of space exploration. Except for the Mercury program, mission patches were designed by the space crews themselves as a way of telling their story. When we hold their patches, we hold a little piece of history. By reading the story the patches tell, we can all take part in the greatest adventure of modern times.

CABANA STURCKOW CURRIE ROSS NEWMAN КРИКАЛЁВ

The STS-88 patch

65

Design Your Own Insignia

You have a story. It is the things you have done, the things you like, the things you dream about, and the things you believe in. Like the crews of the space missions that have begun the exploration of outer space, you can have your own mission patch that tells your story in symbols. At first, designing your own patch seems like a simple job but it is more complicated than you think. You need to sit down and list the parts of the story you want to tell. Not everything will fit and you must make choices. Then, you need to choose the appropriate symbols to represent those parts. After that comes the design process where the parts are fit together. Finally comes the actual creation of the patch with art supplies. Begin your patch by following these steps:

1 List on paper the things you want your patch to tell about you. The list might include your hobbies, sports you like, subjects you find interesting, what you would do if you could do anything you want, and so on.

2 Put a second column on the same piece of paper next to the first and list the symbols that might be used to represent the things in the first column. For example, if you list science as an interest, a microscope might be used. A football could be used for sports. A book could be used for reading. A sailboat could be used for seeking adventure.

3 Decide if you want words on your patch and what those words will be. Your name can be used but you might want a quote on the patch, such as *carpe diem* (seize the day).

4 Decide what shape your patch should be. The shape of the patch is as important as the things found on it. Round patches are good, but a triangle might be used if you want to show three important things. An upward slanting oval can be used to give a sense of flight. The patch can be the shape of a rocket or a car.

5 Make several different pencil sketches of your patch. Put the most important symbols on your patch first and then try to fit the less important ones in. You may have to drop a few.

6 Stick your sketches up on a wall and look at them for a couple of days. You will probably find some more to your liking, or you may come up with new ideas. Finally, pick the patch that appeals to you the most.

7 Sketch your chosen patch again, but this time add color to it and try different combinations. If you can do this with an art program on a computer, you can quickly switch colors to try different combinations.

You will find that certain colors do not work together. Dark purple letters, for example, do not stand out very well on a black background but yellow or white letters will. Unless you plan to have decals professionally printed, you do not have to be concerned with the number of colors you use.

8 When you finally pick your patch design, create one from cloth. If you know someone who does embroidery on a sewing machine, ask that person to make the patch for you. Another way to make the patch is to buy some cloth at a fabric or craft store and a selection of colored fabric glues. The glues produce a bead of rubbery color that can be used for

drawing pictures on cloth. Lightly draw your design on the fabric with pencil and then add the colors. Be sure to make a border around the patch in glue. When you cut out the patch, the glue will keep the fabric from fraying.

9 The last step is to cut out your patch and attach it to a piece of clothing. Sew it on to a jacket or a shirt. Use the same color of thread as the patch border to hide the threads.

The Real Mercury Symbols

None of the Mercury flights had mission patches as we know them today. Instead, the name of the space capsule was painted on one side panel to the left of the entry hatch.

Mercury Redstone 3 — *Freedom 7*
Alan B. Shepard Jr. added the number 7 to the name *Freedom* because his spacecraft was factory model 7. The other astronauts felt the number 7 would better represent the number of astronauts in the Mercury program and also added 7 to their spacecraft names.

Mercury Redstone 4 — *Liberty Bell 7*
Virgil I. Grissom liked the name *Liberty Bell* because the capsule was bell-shaped and the Liberty Bell was an important artifact of America's history.

Mercury Atlas 6 — *Friendship 7*
John H. Glenn Jr.'s entire family was put to work to select the name for his capsule. He felt that naming the capsule *Friendship* would be a good message for the people of all the countries he planned to fly over.

Mercury Atlas 7 — *Aurora 7*

Scott Carpenter chose the name *Aurora* because of its significance to space and because he lived on the corner of Aurora and 7th Street when he was a child in Colorado.

Mercury Atlas 8 — *Sigma 7*

Walter M. Schirra Jr. picked *Sigma* as his capsule name because it is a mathematical symbol meaning "sum of." His flight was the sum of many people working together.

Mercury Atlas 9 — *Faith 7*

L. Gordon Cooper Jr. decided to name his capsule *Faith* because it showed his faith in his fellow workers.

THE REAL NASA INSIGNIA

NASA's meatball insignia has had its ups and downs. It was designed by James Modarelli, a NASA employee, when the agency was created in 1959. Modarelli designed both NASA's official seal (for documents and official functions) and the insignia for everyday use. The insignia was based on the design for the seal. Modarelli said, "I chose the main elements from the seal—the sphere, representing a planet; stars, representing space; the wing, representing aeronautics; and an orbiting spacecraft. Then I added the letters: NASA." The wing on the insignia (red sideways V) was based on a design for an advanced high-speed aircraft wing that was currently being tested.

The NASA insignia was added to every astronaut flight suit from the Mercury missions through Apollo. In 1986, the insignia was changed to a trendy new design that featured the letters N-A-S-A in flowing red letters on a white background. The insignia was quickly dubbed the "worm" and it made many NASA employees unhappy. Someone suggested combining the two insignias by replacing the letters on the meatball with the letters from the worm. The new concept, which was never adopted, was nicknamed the "wormball."

The NASA "worm" patch

In 1992, NASA Administrator Daniel S. Goldin decided to return to the NASA meatball insignia. Newer NASA employees were unhappy with the change but the old-timers were elated. The insignia remains the meatball today, even though small modifications are occasionally made. The original white circular border of the insignia was changed to royal blue for the Apollo program. The red wing officially extends in both directions off the insignia but some patches have shown the wing within the blue border of the circle. Presumably, this was done to make the patch easier to manufacture.

Glossary

Apollo Project—the United States space program that sent teams of three astronauts to the Moon and back.

Apollo-Soyuz—the mid-1970 space flight that linked an American Apollo spacecraft with a Soviet Soyuz spacecraft in orbit.

Command Module—the capsule portion of the Apollo spacecraft.

Extravehicular Activity (EVA)—space walking.

Gemini Project—second United States space program, in which teams of two astronauts learned how to rendezvous and dock spacecraft in orbit and to space walk.

International Space Station—a space station currently under construction in Earth orbit.

Mercury Project—first manned space missions for the United States in which individual astronauts demonstrated that humans could live and work in space and return safely to Earth.

Mission Patch (Insignia)—a cloth patch with symbols representing the goals of a particular space mission.

National Aeronautics and Space Administration (NASA)—the American space agency.

Saturn V rocket—the launch vehicle used for sending astronauts to the Moon and for launching Skylab.

Service module—the rocket propulsion, electric power, and water and oxygen supply vehicle for the Apollo spacecraft.

Skylab—the first space station launched by the United States.

Space shuttle—reusable space vehicle currently being used by NASA for its crewed space missions.

Unity—the American node for connecting modules to the International Space Station.

Zarya—the Russian Functional Cargo Block (FGB) for the International Space Station.

FOR FURTHER INFORMATION

Lattimer, Dick. *All We Did Was Fly to the Moon*. Gainesville, FL: The Whispering Eagle Press, 1985.

Neal, Valerie, Cathleen Lewis, and Frank Winter. *Spaceflight: A Smithsonian Guide*. Washington, DC: IDG Books Worldwide, Smithsonian Institution, 1995.

Pictures of NASA Patches
http://www.hq.nasa.gov/office/pao/History/mission_patches.html

Summaries of NASA spaceflight
http://www.spaceline.org/shuttlechron.html

Sources for NASA Patches:
http://www.nasapatches.com/
http://www.premierespace.com/index.htm
http://www.spaceage-collectibles.com/spaceage/patcat.htm
http://www.military-patches.com/index.htm#search

NASA patches can also be obtained from visitor center stores at NASA installations and at many science museums.

Index

Published by The Millbrook Press
2 Old New Milford Road
Brookfield, Connecticut 06804
www.millbrookpress.com
Copyright © 2001 by Gregory L. Vogt
Printed in Hong Kong

Cover and interior photographs courtesy of NASA

Library of Congress Cataloging-in-Publication Data
Vogt, Gregory.
Space mission patches/by Gregory L. Vogt.
p. cm.
Includes index.
ISBN 0-7613-1613-2 (lib. bdg.)
1. Astronautics—United States—Collectibles—Juvenile literature. 2. United States.
National Aeronautics and Space Administration—Insignia—Juvenile literature. 3. Manned
space flight—Collectibles—Juvenile literature. 4. Astronauts—United
States—Collectibles—Juvenile literature. 5. Badges—United States—Collectibles—Juvenile
literature. [1. Space flights. 2. Astronautics. 3. United States. National Aeronautics and
Space Administration—Insignia.] I. Title.
TL789.8.U5 V54 2001   629.45′002′75—dc21   00-041850